Presented To:

_____

From:

_____

Date:

_____

*For this reason He had to be made like His brothers
in every way, in order that He might become
a merciful and faithful high priest.*

HEBREWS 2:17

·

December 31

Words

Tell your children how great their mother or father is.
Do this behind your spouse's back and in her presence.

December 30

Keeping love alive in our marriages is serious business.

January 1

Jesus went through all the towns and villages,
teaching in their synagogues, preaching the good news
of the kingdom and healing every disease and sickness.
When He saw the crowds, He had compassion on them.

MATTHEW 9:35, 36

December 29

Love one another. As I have loved you,
so you must love one another.

JOHN 13:34

January 2

Gifts

Give a living gift. Purchase and plant a tree or flowering shrub
in honor of your spouse. You may plant it in your own yard,
where you can water and nurture it, or with permission
in a public park or forest where others can also enjoy it.
You will get credit for this one year after year.

December 28

Most of us grow up learning the language of our parents and siblings, which becomes our primary or native tongue. Later we may learn additional languages—but usually with much more effort. These become our secondary languages. We speak and understand best our native language. We feel most comfortable speaking that language. The more we use a secondary language, the more comfortable we become conversing in it.

January 3

The Lord is good to all;
He has compassion on all He has made.

PSALM 145:9

December 27

Her children arise and call her blessed;
her husband also, and he praises her.

PROVERBS 31:28

January 4

Service

I vacuum our house regularly. There is only one reason
I vacuum our house. Love. You couldn't pay me enough
to vacuum a house, but I do it for love. You see,
when an action doesn't come naturally to you, it is a greater
expression of love. My wife knows that when I vacuum
the house, it's nothing but 100 percent pure,
unadulterated love, and I get credit for the whole thing!

December 26

Gifts

A gift is something you can hold in your hand and say,
"Look, he was thinking of me," or "She remembered me."

January 5

The Lord is gracious and compassionate,
slow to anger and rich in love.

PSALM 145:8

December 25

Encourage one another and build each other up.

I THESSALONIANS 5:11

January 6

Touch

When your spouse arrives at home, meet him or her
one step earlier than usual and give your mate
a big welcome home. The point is to vary the routine
and enhance even a small "touching experience."

December 24

Touch

We have long known that physical touch is a way of communicating emotional love. Numerous research projects in the area of child development have reached that conclusion: Babies who are held, hugged, and kissed develop a healthier emotional life than those who are left for long periods of time without physical contact.

January 7

Glorious and majestic are His deeds,
and His righteousness endures forever.
He has caused His wonders to be remembered;
the Lord is gracious and compassionate.

PSALM 111:3, 4

December 23

Neither height nor depth, nor anything else in all creation,
will be able to separate us from the love of God
that is in Christ Jesus our Lord.

ROMANS 8:39

January 8

Do you think by now you have a good sense of what your spouse's love language is? How about them for you? What more could you do to explore this?

December 22

Your emotional love language and the language
of your spouse may be as different as Chinese from English.
No matter how hard you try to express love in English,
if your spouse understands only Chinese, you will never
understand how to love each other.

January 9

But You, O Lord, are a compassionate and gracious God,
slow to anger, abounding in love and faithfulness.

PSALM 86:15

December 21

Time

When I sit with my wife and give her twenty minutes
of my undivided attention and she does the same for me,
we are giving each other twenty minutes of life.
We will never have those twenty minutes again;
we are giving our lives to each other.
It is a powerful emotional communicator of love.

January 10

Words

Look for your spouse's strengths and tell her how much
you appreciate those strengths. Chances are she will
work hard to live up to her reputation.

December 20

Words

Mark Twain once said, "I can live for two months
on a good compliment." If we take Twain literally,
six compliments a year would have kept
his emotional love tank at the operational level.
Your spouse will probably need more.

January 11

Because of the Lord's great love we are not consumed,
for His compassions never fail.

LAMENTATIONS 3:22

December 19

There is a time for everything,
and a season for every activity
under heaven…a time to love.

ECCLESIASTES 3:1, 8

January 12

If you have not discovered your primary love language, keep records on the Tank Check game. When your spouse says, "What could I do to help fill your tank?" your suggestions will likely cluster around your primary love language. You may request things from all five love languages, but you will have more requests centering on your primary love language.

December 18

Language differences are part and parcel of human culture. If we are to communicate effectively across cultural lines, we must learn the language of those with whom we wish to communicate.

January 13

For the Lord is good and His love endures forever;
His faithfulness continues through all generations.

PSALM 100:5

December 17

Continue to live in Him, rooted and built up in Him,
strengthened in the faith as you were taught,
and overflowing with thankfulness.

COLOSSIANS 2:7

January 14

Gifts

Give a lasting tribute. Give a gift to your spouse's church or favorite charity in honor of her birthday, your anniversary, or another occasion. Ask the charity to send a card informing your spouse of what you have done. The church or charity will be excited and so will your spouse.

December 16

There are five emotional love languages—five ways that people speak and understand emotional love.

January 15

The Lord is full of compassion and mercy.

JAMES 5:11

December 15

Every good and perfect gift is from above,
coming down from the Father of the heavenly lights,
who does not change like shifting shadows.

JAMES 1:17

January 16

Play the "Tank Check" game three times a week
for three weeks. When you come home, one of you says
to the other, "On a scale of zero to ten, how is your
love tank tonight?" Zero means empty, and ten means
"I am full of love and can't handle any more." You give
a reading on your emotional love tank—10, 9, 8, 7, 6, 5,
4, 3, 2, 1, or 0, indicating how full it is. Your spouse says,
"What could I do to help fill it?"

December 14

Could it be that gift giving is a fundamental expression of love that transcends cultural barriers? Is the attitude of love always accompanied by the concept of giving? Those are academic and somewhat philosophical questions, but if the answer is yes, it has profound practical implications for North American couples.

January 17

May all who seek You rejoice and be glad in You;
may those who love Your salvation always say,
"Let God be exalted!"

PSALM 70:4

December 13

Gifts

*This is love: not that we loved God,
but that He loved us and sent His Son
as an atoning sacrifice for our sins.*

I JOHN 4:10

January 18

Touch

When family or friends are visiting, touch your spouse
in their presence. Putting your arm around him as you stand
talking, or simply placing your hand on her shoulder says,
"Even with all these people in our house, I still see you."

December 12

Time

It isn't enough to just be in the same room with someone.
A key ingredient in giving your spouse quality time
is giving them focused attention, especially in this era
of many distractions.

January 19

I will betroth you in righteousness and justice,
in love and compassion.

HOSEA 2:19

December 11

*How great is the love the Father has lavished on us,
that we should be called children of God!*

I JOHN 3:1

January 20

Spend some time writing down what you think is your primary love language. Then list the other four in order of importance. Also write down what you think is the primary love language of your spouse. You may also list the other four in order of importance if you wish. Sit down with your spouse and discuss what you guessed to be his/her primary love language. Then tell each other what you consider to be your own primary love language.

December 10

Service

Acts of service means doing things you know your spouse would like you to do. You seek to please her by serving her, to express your love for her by doing things for her.

January 21

I will tell of the kindnesses of the Lord,
the deeds for which He is to be praised...
according to His compassion and many kindnesses.

ISAIAH 63:7

December 9

Words

One way to express love emotionally is to use words
that build up. Solomon, author of the ancient
Hebrew Wisdom Literature, wrote,
"The tongue has the power of life and death."

January 22

Time

Camp out in the living room. Spread your blankets
and pillows on the floor. Get your Pepsi and popcorn.
Pretend the TV is broken and talk like you used to when you
were dating. Talk till the sun comes up or something
else happens. If the floor gets too hard, go back upstairs
and go to bed. You won't forget this evening!

December 8

This is how we know what love is:
Jesus Christ laid down His life for us.

I JOHN 3:16

January 23

Let the morning bring me word of Your unfailing love,
for I have put my trust in You.

PSALM 143:8

December 7

Touch

Physical touch is a powerful vehicle for communicating
marital love. Holding hands, kissing, embracing,
and sexual intercourse are all ways of communicating
emotional love to one's spouse.

January 24

Words

Compliment your spouse in the presence of his parents or friends. You will get double credit: Your spouse will feel loved and the parents will feel lucky to have such a great son-in-law or daughter-in-law.

December 6

And so we know and rely on the love God has for us.
God is love. Whoever lives in love lives in God,
and God in him.

I JOHN 4:16

January 25

I will bow down toward Your holy temple
and will praise Your name
for Your love and Your faithfulness.

PSALM 138:2

December 5

There are not 10, 20, or 365 basic love languages. In my opinion, there are only five. However, there may be numerous dialects. The number of ways to express love within a love language is limited only by one's imagination. The important thing is to speak the love language of your spouse.

January 26

Service

Ask your spouse to tell you the daily acts of service
that would really speak love to him or her.
Seek to work these into your daily schedule.
"Little things" really do mean a lot.

December 4

Love the Lord your God will all your heart
and with all your soul and with all your strength.

DEUTERONOMY 6:5

January 27

Preserve my life according to Your love,
and I will obey the statutes of Your mouth.

PSALM 119:88

December 3

Being sincere is not enough. We must be willing to learn our spouse's primary love language if we are to be effective communicators of love.

January 28

Ask yourself, "What would be an ideal spouse to me?
If I could have the perfect mate, what would she be like?"
Your picture of a perfect mate should give you some idea
of your primary love language.

December 2

There is no fear in love. But perfect love drives out fear.

I JOHN 4:18

January 29

Whoever is wise, let him...consider the great love of the Lord.

PSALM 107:43

December 1

Time

Quality time does not mean that we have to spend
our together moments gazing into each other's eyes.
It means that we are doing something together
and that we are giving our full attention to the other person.

January 30

Gifts

Give your spouse a book and agree to read it yourself.
Then offer to discuss together a chapter each week.
Don't choose a book that you want him or her to read.
Choose a book on a topic in which you know your spouse
has an interest: sex, football, needlework,
money management, child rearing, religion, backpacking.

November 30

This is how God showed His love among us:
He sent His one and only Son into the world
that we might live through Him.

I JOHN 4:9

January 31

He redeems my life from the pit
and crowns me with love and compassion.

PSALM 103:4

November 29

Gifts

You must be thinking of someone to give him a gift.
The gift itself is a symbol of that thought.
It doesn't matter whether it costs money.
What is important is that you thought of him.
And it is not the thought implanted only in the mind
that counts, but the thought expressed in actually
securing the gift and giving it as the expression of love.

February 1

Two kinds of people may have difficulty discovering their primary love language. The first is the individual whose emotional love tank has been full for a long time. The second is the individual whose love tank has been empty for so long that he doesn't remember what makes him feel loved. In either case, go back to the experience of falling in love and ask yourself, "What did I like about my spouse in those days?

November 28

Words

Many couples have never learned the tremendous power
of verbally affirming each other. Solomon noted,
"An anxious heart weighs a man down,
but a kind word cheers him up."

February 2

It is good to praise the Lord and make music to Your name,
O Most High, to proclaim Your love in the morning
and Your faithfulness at night.

PSALM 92:1, 2

November 27

In the field of linguistics a language may have numerous dialects or variations. Similarly, within the five basic emotional love languages, there are many dialects. That accounts for the magazine articles titled "10 Ways to Let Your Spouse Know You Love Her," "20 Ways to Keep Your Man at Home," or "365 Expressions of Marital Love."

February 3

Time

Have a "Let's review our history" evening once every three months. Set aside an hour to focus on your history. Select five questions each of you will answer. Each evening, agree on your five questions before you begin your sharing. At the end of the five questions, stop and decide on the five questions you will ask next time.

November 26

Touch

For some individuals, physical touch is their
primary love language. Without it, they feel unloved.
With it, their emotional tank is filled,
and they feel secure in the love of their spouse.

February 4

Because Your love is better than life,
my lips will glorify You.

PSALM 63:3

November 25

Keep yourselves in God's love.

JUDE 21

February 5

Touch

Initiate sex by giving your spouse a foot massage.
Continue to other parts of the body
as long as it brings pleasure to your spouse.

November 24

Love need not evaporate after the wedding, but in order to keep it alive most of us will have to put forth the effort to learn a secondary love language. We cannot rely on our native tongue if our spouse does not understand it. If we want them to feel the love we are trying to communicate, we must express it in his or her primary love language.

February 6

Words

Write a love letter, a love paragraph, or a love sentence
to your spouse, and give it quietly or with fanfare!
You may someday find your love letter tucked away
in some special place. Words are important!

November 23

*Love comes from God. Everyone who loves
has been born of God and knows God.*

I JOHN 4:7

February 7

Within Your temple, O God,
we meditate on Your unfailing love.

PSALM 48:9

November 22

Time

A husband and wife playing tennis together, if it is
genuine quality time, will focus not on the game
but on the fact that they are spending time together.
What happens on the emotional level is what matters.
Our spending time together in a common pursuit
communicates that we care about each other, that we enjoy
being with each other, that we like to do things together.

February 8

If two languages seem to be equal for you, that is,
both speak loudly to you, then perhaps you are bilingual.
If so, you make it easier on your spouse.
Now he or she has two choices, either of which
will strongly communicate love to you.

November 21

*For God so loved the world that He gave
His one and only Son, that whoever believes in Him
shall not perish but have eternal life.*

JOHN 3:16

February 9

Have mercy on me, O God,
according to Your unfailing love;
according to Your great compassion.

PSALM 51:1

November 20

Complete the following: "There would be fewer divorces if only people _____ ."

February 10

In what way do you regularly express love to your spouse?
Your method of expressing love may be an indication
that that would also make you feel loved.

November 19

Service

Such actions as cooking a meal, setting a table, washing dishes, vacuuming, cleaning a commode, changing the baby's diaper, dusting the bookcase, keeping the car in operating condition, paying the bills, trimming the shrubs, walking the dog, changing the cat's litter box, and dealing with landlords and insurance companies are all acts of service. They require thought, planning, time, effort, and energy. If done with a positive spirit, they are indeed expressions of love.

February 11

By day the Lord directs His love,
at night His song is with me.

PSALM 42:8

November 18

I have loved you with an everlasting love;
I have drawn you with lovingkindness.

JEREMIAH 31:3

February 12

Gifts

Offer the gift of presence. Say to your spouse, "I want
to offer the gift of my presence at any event or on any occasion
you would like this month. You tell me when, and I will
make every effort to be there." Get ready! Be positive!
Who knows, you may enjoy the symphony or the hockey game.

November 17

Words

Verbal compliments, or words of appreciation, are powerful communicators of love. They are best expressed in simple, straightforward statements of affirmation.

February 13

May Your love and Your truth always protect me.

PSALM 40:11

November 16

Gifts

Mothers remember the days their children bring a flower
from the yard as a gift. They feel loved, even if it was
a flower they didn't want picked. From early years,
children are inclined to give gifts to their parents,
which may be another indication that gift giving
is fundamental to love.

February 14

Time

Make time every day to share with each other
some of the events of the day. When you spend more time
on Facebook than you do listening to each other,
you can end up more concerned about your hundred
"friends" than about your spouse.

November 15

Once you identify and learn to speak your spouse's primary love language, I believe that you will have discovered the key to a long-lasting, loving marriage.

February 15

I do not hide Your righteousness in my heart;
I speak of Your faithfulness and salvation.
I do not conceal Your love and Your truth.

PSALM 40:10

November 14

And we know that in all things God works
for the good of those who love Him,
who have been called according to His purpose.

ROMANS 8:28

February 16

Words

As you watch TV, read, or listen to people's conversations, look for words of affirmation that people use. Write those affirming statements in a notebook or keep them electronically. Read through these periodically and select those you could use with your spouse. When you use one, note the date on which you used it. Your notebook may become your love book. Remember, words are important!

November 13

Touch

Of the five senses, touching, unlike the other four,
is not limited to one localized area of the body. Tiny tactile
receptors are located throughout the body. When those
receptors are touched or pressed, nerves carry impulses
to the brain. The brain interprets these impulses
and we perceive that the thing that touched us is warm
or cold, hard or soft. It causes pain or pleasure.
We may also interpret it as loving or hostile.

February 17

For with You is the fountain of life;
in Your light we see light.
Continue Your love to those who know You.

PSALM 36:9, 10

November 12

Who shall separate us from the love of Christ?

ROMANS 8:35

February 18

Service

If you have more money than time, hire someone to do the acts of service that you know your spouse would like for you to do, such as the yard work or a once-a-month deep cleaning of your home.

November 11

Time

One of the most common dialects is that of
quality conversation. By quality conversation,
I mean sympathetic dialogue where two individuals
are sharing their experiences, thoughts, feelings,
and desires in a friendly, uninterrupted context.

February 19

Touch

When you sit together in church, when the minister calls
for prayer, reach over and hold your spouse's hand.

November 10

We are more than conquerors through Him who loved us.

ROMANS 8:37

February 20

What have you most often requested of your spouse?
The thing you have most often requested is likely the thing
that would make you feel most loved.

November 9

Psychologists have concluded that the need to feel loved is a primary human emotional need. For love, we will climb mountains, cross seas, traverse desert sands, and endure untold hardships. Without love, mountains become unclimbable, seas uncrossable, deserts unbearable, and hardships our lot in life.

February 21

How priceless is Your unfailing love!
Both high and low among men find refuge
in the shadow of Your wings.

PSALM 36:7

November 8

*Nothing...in all creation, will be able to separate us
from the love of God that is in Christ Jesus our Lord.*

ROMANS 8:39

February 22

What does your spouse do or fail to do that hurts you most deeply? The opposite of what hurts you most is probably your love language.

November 7

Words

Verbal compliments are far greater motivators
than nagging words.

February 23

For Your love is ever before me.

PSALM 26:3

November 6

His banner over me is love.

SONG OF SOLOMON 2:4

February 24

Time

Plan a weekend getaway just for the two of you
sometime within the next six months. Be sure it is
a weekend when you won't have to call the office or have
a commitment with your kids. Focus on relaxing together
doing what one or both of you enjoy.

November 5

Love is the most important word in the English language—and the most confusing. Both secular and religious thinkers agree that love plays a central role in life.

February 25

Remember, O Lord, Your great mercy and love,
for they are from of old....
According to Your love remember me,
for You are good, O Lord.

PSALM 25:6, 7

November 4

The Lord your God is with you, He is mighty to save.
He will take great delight in you, He will quiet you
with His love, He will rejoice over you with singing.

ZEPHANIAH 3:17

February 26

Discovering the primary love language of your spouse
is essential if you are to keep their emotional love tank full.

November 3

Gifts

Gifts are visual symbols of love. Most wedding ceremonies include the giving and receiving of rings. The person performing the ceremony says, "These rings are outward and visible signs of an inward and spiritual bond that unites your two hearts in love that has no end." That is not meaningless rhetoric. It is verbalizing a significant truth— symbols have emotional value.

February 27

Show the wonder of Your great love,
You who save by Your right hand....
Keep me as the apple of Your eye.

PSALM 17:7, 8

November 2

The emotional need for love…is fundamental to our nature.
It is at the center of our emotional desires.
We needed love before we "fell in love,"
and we will need it as long as we live.

February 28

Gifts

Enlist a "personal shopper." If you really don't have a clue as to how to select a gift for your spouse, ask a friend or family member who knows your wife or husband well to help you. Most people enjoy making a friend happy by getting them a gift, especially if it is with your money.

November 1

Time

Most individuals who complain that their spouse does not talk do not mean literally that he or she never says a word. They mean that he or she seldom takes part in sympathetic dialogue. If your spouse's primary love language is quality time, such dialogue is crucial to his or her emotional sense of being loved.

February 29

Whatever is lovely...think about such things.

PHILIPPIANS 4:8

October 31

As the Father has loved Me, so have I loved you.
Now remain in My love.

JOHN 15:9

March 1

Words

Set a goal to give your spouse a different compliment each day for one month. If "an apple a day keeps the doctor away," maybe a compliment a day will keep the counselor away. (You may want to record these compliments also, so you will not duplicate the statements.)

October 30

Touch

Some parts of the body are more sensitive than others. The difference is due to the fact that the tiny tactile receptors are not scattered evenly over the body but arranged in clusters. Thus, the tip of the tongue is highly sensitive to touch whereas the back of the shoulders is the least sensitive. The tips of the fingers and the tip of the nose are other extremely sensitive areas. Our purpose, however, is not to understand the neurological basis of the sense of touch but rather its psychological importance.

March 2

When the kindness and love of God our Savior appeared,
He saved us, not because of righteous things we had done,
but because of His mercy.

TITUS 3:4, 5

October 29

Service

No one likes to be forced to do anything. In fact,
love is always freely given. Love cannot be demanded.
We can request things of each other, but we must never
demand anything. Requests give direction to love,
but demands stop the flow of love.

March 3

Expressing love in a person's primary love language
enhances all relationships.

October 28

Something in our nature cries out to be loved by another.

March 4

Touch

While your spouse is seated, walk up behind her
and give her a shoulder massage.

October 27

Greater love has no one than this,
that he lay down his life for his friends.

JOHN 15:13

March 5

Time

Think of an activity your spouse enjoys, but which brings little pleasure to you: NASCAR, browsing in flea markets, working out. Tell your spouse that you are trying to broaden your horizons and would like to join him in this activity sometime this month. Set a date and give it your best effort.

October 26

Words

When we receive affirming words
we are far more likely to be motivated to reciprocate
and do something our spouse desires.

March 6

Be devoted to one another in brotherly love.
Honor one another above yourselves.

ROMANS 12:10

October 25

Righteous Father...I have made You known to them,
and will continue to make You known in order that
the love You have for Me may be in them.

JOHN 17:25, 26

March 7

Can emotional love be reborn in a marriage after many years? Yes, if the two of you are willing to try speaking each other's love language.

October 24

The need to feel loved by one's spouse is at the heart
of marital desires. A man said to me recently,
"What good is the house, the cars, the place at the beach,
or any of the rest of it if your wife doesn't love you?"
Do you understand what he was really saying?
"More than anything, I want to be loved by my wife."
Material things are no replacement for human, emotional love.

March 8

Love must be sincere.

ROMANS 12:9

October 23

And hope does not disappoint us,
because God has poured out His love into our heart
by the Holy Spirit whom He has given us.

ROMANS 5:5

March 9

Words

For one week, keep a written record of all the words of affirmation you give your spouse each day. On Monday, I said: "You did a great job on this meal." "You really look nice in that outfit." "I appreciate your picking up the dry cleaning." On Tuesday, I said: etc. You might be surprised how well (or how poorly) you are speaking words of affirmation.

October 22

Time

Words of affirmation focus on what we are saying,
whereas quality conversation focuses on what we are hearing.

March 10

Service

Perform a major act of service like organizing
the home office, and then post a sign that reads,
"To (spouse's name) with love," and sign your name.

October 21

Gifts

Visual symbols of love are more important to some people than to others. That's why individuals have different attitudes toward wedding rings. Some never take the ring off after the wedding. Others don't even wear a wedding band. That is another sign that people have different primary love languages.

March 11

Gifts

Keep a "Gift Idea Notebook." Every time you hear
your spouse say, "I really like that," write it down
in your notebook. Listen carefully and you will get quite
a list. This will serve as a guide when you get ready
to select a gift. To prime the pump, you could look through
a favorite online shopping site together.

October 20

But God demonstrates His own love for us in this:
While we were still sinners, Christ died for us.

ROMANS 5:8

March 12

There is nothing more powerful that you can do than to love your spouse even when they are not responding positively. Whatever the ultimate response of your spouse, you will have the satisfaction of knowing that you have done everything you could do to restore your marriage. If your spouse eventually chooses to reciprocate your love, you will have demonstrated for yourself the power of unconditional love. And you will reap the benefits of the rebirth of mutual love.

October 19

Marriage is designed to meet that need for intimacy and love. That is why the ancient biblical writings spoke of the husband and wife becoming "one flesh." That did not mean that individuals would lose their identity; it meant that they would enter into each other's lives in a deep and intimate way.

March 13

All of you, live in harmony with one another; be sympathetic, love as brothers, be compassionate and humble.

I PETER 3:8

October 18

He died for all, that those who live
should no longer live for themselves
but for Him who died for them
and was raised again.

II CORINTHIANS 5:15

March 14

Time

Ask your spouse where she most enjoys sitting when talking with you. The next week, text her one afternoon and say, "I want to make a date with you one evening this week to sit on the porch and talk. Which night and what time would be best for you?"

October 17

Physical touch can make or break a relationship.
It can communicate hate or love. To the person
whose primary love language is physical touch,
the message will be far louder than the words
"I hate you" or "I love you."

March 15

In Your love You kept me.

ISAIAH 38:17

October 16

Touch

*Be of one mind, live in peace.
And the God of love and peace
will be with you.*

II CORINTHIANS 13:11

March 16

I believe that our deepest emotional need is the need to feel loved. If we are married, the person we would most like to love us is our spouse. If we feel loved by our spouse, the whole world is bright and life is wonderful.

October 15

Words

The word *encourage* means "to inspire courage."
All of us have areas in which we feel insecure.
We lack courage, and that lack of courage often hinders us
from accomplishing the positive things that we would like
to do. The latent potential within your spouse in his or her
areas of insecurity may await your encouraging words.

March 17

The Father Himself loves you because you have loved Me.

JOHN 16:27

October 14

Understanding the five love languages and learning
to speak the primary love language of your spouse
may radically affect his or her behavior. People behave
differently when their emotional love tanks are full.

March 18

Touch

Walk up to your spouse and say, "Have I told you lately
that I love you?" Take her in your arms and hug her
while you rub her back and continue. "You are the greatest!"
(Resist the temptation to rush to the bedroom.)
Untangle yourself and move on to the next thing.

October 13

May the grace of the Lord Jesus Christ, and the love of God, and the fellowship of the Holy Spirit be with you all.

II CORINTHIANS 13:14

March 19

To Him who loves us and has freed us
from our sins by His blood.

REVELATION 1:5

October 12

Time

Marriage is a relationship, not a project to be completed
or a problem to solve. A relationship calls for
sympathetic listening with a view to understanding
the other person's thoughts, feelings, and desires.

March 20

Words

To remind yourself that "Words of Affirmation"
are important, print the following on a 3x5 card and put it
on a mirror or other place where you will see it daily:

Words are important!
Words are important!
Words are important!

October 11

The fruit of the Spirit is love, joy, peace, patience, kindness, goodness, faithfulness, gentleness, and self-control.

GALATIANS 5:22, 23

March 21

Any one of these love languages can be the primary love language of a man or the primary love language of a woman. The important thing in marriage is that you discover the primary and secondary love languages of your spouse and you speak these regularly. If you do this, you will create a healthy emotional climate for marital growth.

October 10

I am convinced that keeping the emotional love tank full is as important to a marriage as maintaining the proper oil level is to an automobile. Running your marriage on an empty "love tank" may cost you even more than trying to drive your car without oil.

March 22

This is love for God: to obey His commands.
And His commands are not burdensome.

I JOHN 5:3

October 9

In love He predestined us to be adopted
as His sons through Jesus Christ.

EPHESIANS 1:4-5

March 23

Gifts

Give your spouse a gift every day for one week. It need not be a special week, just any week. I promise you it will become "The Week That Was!" If you are really energetic, you can make it "The Month That Was!" No—your spouse will not expect you to keep this up for a lifetime.

October 8

Service

Each of us must decide daily to love or not to love our spouses. If we choose to love, then expressing it in the way in which our spouse requests will make our love most effective emotionally.

March 24

Since God so loved us, we also ought to love one another.

I JOHN 4:11

October 7

Gifts

If receiving gifts is my primary love language, I will place great value on the ring you have given me and I will wear it with great pride. I will also be greatly moved emotionally by other gifts that you give through the years. I will see them as expressions of love. Without gifts as visual symbols, I may question your love.

March 25

Time

Ask your spouse for a list of five activities that he would
enjoy doing with you. Make plans to do one of them
each month for the next five months. If money is a problem,
space the freebies between the "we can't afford this" events.

October 6

Has there ever been a time when you did something because you "meant well"—that is, out of loving motives? How did it turn out?

March 26

Dear children, let us not love with words or tongue
but with actions and in truth.

I JOHN 3:18

October 5

Because of His great love for us,
God, who is rich in mercy,
made us alive with Christ.

EPHESIANS 2:4, 5

March 27

All of the five love languages can be learned. It is true that most of us grew up speaking only one or two of these love languages. These will come natural for us and will be relatively easy. The others must be learned. As in all learning situations, small steps make for big gains.

October 4

Words

Perhaps your spouse has untapped potential in one
or more areas of life. That potential may be awaiting
your encouraging words. Perhaps she needs to enroll
in a course to develop that potential. Maybe he needs
to meet some people who have succeeded in that area,
who can give him insight on the next step he needs to take.
Your words may give your spouse the courage necessary
to take that first step.

March 28

If anyone loves the world, the love of the Father is not in him.

I JOHN 2:15

October 3

*Peace to the brothers, and love with faith
from God the Father and the Lord Jesus Christ.*

EPHESIANS 6:23

March 29

Though our spouse's complaints normally irritate us, they are actually giving us valuable information. If a spouse says, "We don't ever spend any time together," you may be tempted to say, "What do you mean? We went out to dinner Thursday night." Such a defensive statement will end the conversation. However, if you respond, "What would you like for us to do?" you will likely get an answer. The complaints of your spouse are the most powerful indicators of their primary love language.

October 2

Time

Most of us have little training in listening.
We are far more efficient in thinking and speaking.
Learning to listen may be as difficult
as learning a foreign language, but learn we must,
if we want to communicate love.

March 30

Whoever loves his brother lives in the light,
and there is nothing in him to make him stumble.

I JOHN 2:10

October 1

Touch

In marriage, the touch of love may take many forms.
Since touch receptors are located throughout the body,
lovingly touching your spouse almost anywhere
can be an expression of love.

March 31

Words

Share instances with your spouse when words
had a profound impact on your life—
positively or negatively.

September 30

"Real love" is emotional in nature but not obsessional.
It is a love that unites reason and emotion.
It involves an act of the will and requires discipline,
and it recognizes the need for personal growth.

April 1

Service

If your requests to your mate come across as nags or putdowns, try writing them in words that would be less offensive to them. Share this revised wording with your spouse. For example, "The yard always looks so nice, and I really appreciate your work. I'd love to thank you in advance for mowing the lawn this week before Julie and Ben come over for dinner." Your husband might even respond: "Where's the lawn mower, I can't wait!" Try it and see.

September 29

I prayed that you, being rooted and established in love,
may have power…to grasp how wide and long
and high and deep is the love of Christ.

EPHESIANS 3:17, 18

April 2

Touch

While eating together, let your knee or foot
drift over and touch your spouse.

September 28

May you…know this love that surpasses knowledge—
that you may be filled to the measure of all the fullness of God.

EPHESIANS 3:19

April 3

A number of years ago, as I faced my own marital struggles, I rediscovered my spiritual roots. Having been raised in the Christian tradition, I reexamined the life of Christ. When I heard Him praying for those who were killing Him, "Father, forgive them, for they know not what they do," I knew that I wanted that kind of love. I committed my life to Him and have found that He provides the inner spiritual energy to love, even when love is not reciprocated.

September 27

Some couples believe that the end of the in-love experience means they have only two options: resign themselves to a life of misery with their spouse, or jump ship and try again. Research seems to indicate that there is a better alternative: We can recognize the in-love experience for what it was—a temporary emotional high—and now pursue "real love" with our spouse.

April 4

Time

Go to the city park and rent bicycles.
Ride until you are tired, then sit and watch the ducks.
When you get tired of the quacks, roll on to the rose garden.
Learn each other's favorite color of rose and why.

September 26

From Him the whole body,
joined and held together
by every supporting ligament,
grows and builds itself up in love.

EPHESIANS 4:16

April 5

Now that you have purified yourselves by obeying the truth
so that you have sincere love for your brothers,
love one another deeply, from the heart.

I PETER 1:22

September 25

Gifts

Gifts come in all sizes, colors, and shapes.
Some are expensive, and others are free.
To the individual whose primary love language
is receiving gifts, the cost of the gift will matter little.

April 6

Gifts

Discover the value of "handmade originals." Make a gift
for your spouse. This may require you to enroll in a class:
ceramics, silversmithing, painting, wood carving, etc.
Your main purpose for enrolling is to make your spouse
a gift. A handmade gift often becomes a family heirloom.

September 24

Be imitators of God, therefore, as dearly loved children
and live a life of love, just as Christ loved us.

EPHESIANS 5:1-2

April 7

Though you have not seen Him, you love Him;
and even though you do not see Him now, you believe in Him
and are filled with an inexpressible and glorious joy.

I PETER 1:8

September 23

Words

Encouragement requires empathy
and seeing the world from your spouse's perspective.
We must first learn what is important to our spouse.
Only then can we give encouragement.

April 8

With empty love tanks, couples tend to argue and withdraw, and some may tend to be violent verbally or physically in their arguments. But when the love tank is full, we create a climate of friendliness, a climate that seeks to understand, that is willing to allow differences and to negotiate problems. I am convinced that no single area of marriage affects the rest of marriage as much as meeting the emotional need for love.

September 22

Time

Maintain eye contact when your spouse is talking.
That keeps your mind from wandering and communicates
that he/she has your full attention.

April 9

Blessed is the man who perseveres under trial,
because when he has stood the test,
he will receive the crown of life
that God has promised to those who love Him.

JAMES 1:12

September 21

Our most basic emotional need is not to fall in love
but to be genuinely loved by another, to know a love
that grows out of reason and choice, not instinct.
I need to be loved by someone who chooses to love me,
who sees in me something worth loving.

April 10

Words

When you are given public honor for an accomplishment,
be sure to share the credit with your spouse.
You may also try your hand at writing words of affirmation.
Written words have the benefit of being read over and over again.

September 20

This is my prayer: that your love may abound more and more in knowledge and depth of insight, so that you may be able to discern what is best.

PHILIPPIANS 1:9-10

April 11

Do not make light of the Lord's discipline,
and do not lose heart when He rebukes you,
because the Lord disciplines those He loves.

HEBREWS 12:5, 6

September 19

"Real love" requires effort and discipline. It is the choice to expend energy in an effort to benefit the other person, knowing that if his or her life is enriched by your effort, you too will find a sense of satisfaction—the satisfaction of having genuinely loved another.

April 12

We each come to marriage with a different personality and history. We bring emotional baggage into our marriage relationship. We come with different expectations, different ways of approaching things, and different opinions about what matters in life. In a healthy marriage, that variety of perspectives must be processed. We need not agree on everything, but we must find a way to handle our differences so that they do not become divisive.

September 18

If you have any encouragement from being united with Christ,
if any comfort from His love…then make my joy complete
by being like-minded, having the same love.

PHILIPPIANS 2:1-2

April 13

May our Lord Jesus Christ Himself and God our Father,
who loved us and by His grace gave us eternal encouragement
and good hope, encourage your hearts and strengthen you
in every good deed and word.

II THESSALONIANS 2:16, 17

September 17

Service

Learning the love language of acts of service
will require some of us to reexamine our stereotypes
of the roles of husbands and wives. These are changing,
but models from our past can linger.

April 14

Time

Take a walk together through the old neighborhood where one of you grew up. Ask questions about your spouse's childhood. Ask, "What are the fun memories of your childhood?" Then, "What was most painful about your childhood?"

September 16

Touch

Not all touches are created equal. Some will bring
more pleasure to your spouse than others.
Your best instructor is your spouse, of course.
After all, she is the one you are seeking to love.
She knows best what she perceives as a loving touch.

April 15

Touch

As you walk from the car to go shopping,
reach out and hold your spouse's hand.

September 15

Give thanks to the Lord, for He is good.
His love endures forever.

PSALM 136:1

April 16

My beloved is mine and I am his.

SONG OF SOLOMON 2:16

September 14

"Real love" does not require the euphoria
of the in-love experience. In fact, true love cannot begin
until the in-love experience has run its course.

April 17

When the emotional need for love is met,
it creates a climate where a couple can deal with
the rest of life in a much more productive manner.

September 13

Since we belong to the day, let us be self-controlled,
putting on faith and love as a breastplate.

I THESSALONIANS 5:8

April 18

Now about brotherly love we do not need to write to you,
for you yourselves have been taught by God to love each other.

I THESSALONIANS 4:9

September 12

Words

With verbal encouragement, we are trying to communicate,
"I know. I care. I am with you. How can I help?" We are
trying to show that we believe in him and in his abilities.
We are giving credit and praise.

April 19

As your marriage grows deeper, make sure you don't ever "rest on your laurels" and forget your spouse's love language and daily needs. You're on the road to your dreams, so stay there! Put appointments into your schedule to assess together how you're doing.

September 11

May the Lord direct your hearts into God's love.

II THESSALONIANS 3:5

April 20

Gifts

Let nature be your guide. The next time you take a walk
through the neighborhood, keep your eyes open for a gift
for your spouse. It may be a stone, a stick, or a feather.
You may even attach special meaning to your natural gift.
For example, a smooth stone may symbolize your marriage
with many of the rough places now polished. A feather may
symbolize how your spouse is the "wind beneath your wings."

September 10

Time

Don't listen to your spouse and do something else
at the same time. Remember, quality time is giving someone
your undivided attention. If you are doing something
you cannot turn from immediately, tell your spouse the truth.
A positive approach might be, "I know you are trying to talk
to me and I'm interested, but I want to give you my
full attention. I can't do that right now, but if you will
give me ten minutes to finish this, I'll sit down and listen
to you." Most spouses will respect such a request.

April 21

Words

Try giving indirect words of affirmation—that is, saying positive things about your spouse when he or she is not present. Eventually, someone will tell your spouse, and you will get full credit for love.

September 9

Pursue righteousness, godliness, faith,
love, endurance and gentleness.

I TIMOTHY 6:11

April 22

Service

What one act of service has your spouse nagged about
consistently? Why not decide to see the nag as a tag?
Your spouse is tagging this as really important to him or her.
If you choose to do it as an expression of love,
it is worth more than a thousand roses.

September 8

Gifts

Gifts may be purchased, found, or made. For the man
who can afford it, you can purchase a beautiful card
for less than five dollars. For the man who cannot,
you can make one for free. Get the paper out
of the trash can where you work, fold it in the middle,
take scissors and cut out a heart, write "I love you,"
and sign your name. Gifts need not be expensive.

April 23

Husbands, love your wives, just as Christ loved the church and gave Himself up for her.

EPHESIANS 5:25

September 7

For God did not give us a spirit of timidity,
but a spirit of power, of love and of self-discipline.

II TIMOTHY 1:7

April 24

Time
___

What in your marriage detracts from spending quality time?

September 6

We cannot take credit for the kind and generous things
we do while under the influence of "the obsession."
We are pushed and carried along by an instinctual force
that goes beyond our normal behavior patterns. But if,
once we return to the real world of human choice,
we choose to be kind and generous, that is real love.

April 25

I have been crucified with Christ and I no longer live,
but Christ lives in me. The life I live in the body, I live by faith
in the Son of God, who loved me and gave Himself for me.

GALATIANS 2:20

September 5

And let us consider how we may spur one another on toward love and good deeds.

HEBREWS 10:24

April 26

When your spouse responds and meets your need,
you will be able to react with not only your will
but your emotions as well. Without overreacting,
continue positive feedback and affirmation
of your spouse at these times.

September 4

The emotional need for love must be met if we are to have emotional health. Married adults long to feel affection and love from their spouses. We feel secure when we are assured that our mate accepts us, wants us, and is committed to our well-being.

April 27

Now these three remain: faith, hope and love.
But the greatest of these is love.

I CORINTHIANS 13:13

September 3

Touch

Learn to speak your spouse's love dialect. Your spouse
may find some touches uncomfortable or irritating.
To insist on continuing those touches is to communicate
the opposite of love. It is saying that you are not sensitive
to her needs and that you care little about her perceptions
of what is pleasant.

April 28

Touch

Recall some nonsexual "touching times"
that enhanced intimacy between the two of you.
What made these times special?

September 2

Time

Listen for feelings. Ask yourself, "What emotion is my spouse experiencing?" When you think you have the answer, confirm it. For example, "It sounds to me like you are feeling disappointed because I forgot." That gives him the chance to clarify his feelings. It also communicates that you are listening intently to what he is saying.

April 29

Love never fails.

I CORINTHIANS 13:8

September 1

Words

Love is kind. If then we are to communicate love verbally,
we must use kind words.

April 30

When you receive positive feedback you know
there is progress. Each month make one nonthreatening
but specific request that is easy for your spouse.
Make sure it relates to your primary love language
and will help replenish your empty tank.

August 31

In the textbook of marriage, the "in-love" stage is but the introduction. The heart of the book is rational, volitional love. That is the kind of love to which the sages have always called us. It is intentional.

May 1

Love...always perseveres.

I CORINTHIANS 13:6, 7

August 30

Gifts

Make a list of all the gifts your spouse has expressed
excitement about receiving through the years. They may be
gifts you have given or gifts given by other family members
or friends. The list will give you an idea of the kind of gifts
your spouse would enjoy receiving.

May 2

Words

If you are not a man or woman of words, if it is not
your primary love language but you think it may be
the love language of your spouse, let me suggest that you
keep a notebook titled "Words of Affirmation."
When you read an article or book on love, record the words
of affirmation you find. When you hear a lecture on love
or you overhear a friend saying something positive about
another person, write it down. In time, you will collect quite
a list of words to use in communicating love to your spouse.

August 29

But if anyone obeys His word,
God's love is truly made complete in him.

I JOHN 2:5

May 3

Love...always hopes.

I CORINTHIANS 13:6, 7

August 28

Service

Learning the primary love language of your spouse
and choosing to speak it makes a tremendous difference
in the emotional climate of a marriage.

May 4

Time

One of the by-products of quality activities
is that they provide a memory bank
from which to draw in the years ahead.

August 27

*This is love: not that we loved God,
but that He loved us and sent His Son
as an atoning sacrifice for our sins.*

I JOHN 4:10

May 5

Gifts

Try a parade of gifts. Leave a box of candy for your spouse
in the morning; have flowers delivered in the afternoon;
give him a gift in the evening. When your spouse asks,
"What is going on?" you respond,
"Just trying to fill your love tank!"

August 26

Words

Most of us have more potential than we will ever develop. What holds us back is often a lack of courage. A loving spouse can supply that all-important catalyst. Of course, encouraging words may be difficult for you to speak. It may not be your primary love language. It may take great effort for you to learn this second language. That will be especially true if you have a pattern of critical and condemning words, but I can assure you that it will be worth the effort.

May 6

Ask how you can be a better spouse, and regardless of the other's attitude, act on what he or she tells you. Continue to both seek more input and comply with those wishes with all your heart and will. Assure your spouse that your motives are pure.

August 25

If love is a choice, then couples have the capacity
to love after the "in-love" obsession has died
and they have returned to the real world. That kind of love
begins with an attitude—a way of thinking.

May 7

I tell you who hear me: Love your enemies, do good to those who hate you, bless those who curse you, pray for those who mistreat you…. Do to others as you would have them do to you. If you love those who love you, what credit is that to you? Even "sinners" love those who love them.

LUKE 6:27-32

August 24

No one has ever seen God; but if we love one another,
God lives in us and His love is made complete in us.

I JOHN 4:12

May 8

Give, and it will be given to you.
A good measure, pressed down,
shaken together and running over,
will be poured into your lap.
For with the measure you use,
it will be measured to you.

LUKE 6:38

August 23

Time

Observe body language. Clenched fists, trembling hands, tears, furrowed brows, and eye movement may give you clues as to what the other is feeling. Sometimes body language speaks one message while words speak another. Ask for clarification to make sure you know what she is really thinking and feeling.

May 9

If your marriage is in serious trouble, you need to begin by making a strong commitment of the will to undertake the following experiment. You risk further pain and rejection, but you also stand to regain a healthy and fulfilling marriage. Count the cost; it's worth the attempt.

August 22

Love is the attitude that says, "I am married to you, and I choose to look out for your interests." Then the one who chooses to love will find appropriate ways to express that decision.

May 10

Love...always trusts.

I CORINTHIANS 13:6, 7

August 21

Words

The manner in which we speak is exceedingly important.
An ancient sage once said, "A soft answer turns away anger."

May 11

Certainly we do not have warm feelings for people who hate us. That would be abnormal, but we can do loving acts for them. That is simply a choice. We hope that such loving acts will have a positive effect upon their attitudes and behavior and treatment, but at least we have chosen to do something positive for them.

August 20

Touch

Sitting close to each other as you watch your favorite television program requires no additional time but may communicate your love loudly. Touching your spouse as you walk through the room where he is sitting takes only a moment. Touching each other when you leave the house and again when you return may involve only a brief kiss or hug but will speak volumes to your spouse.

May 12

Touch

Crises provide a unique opportunity for expressing love.
Your tender touches will be remembered long after the crisis
has passed. Your failure to touch may never be forgotten.

August 19

God is love.
Whoever lives in love lives in God,
and God in him.

I JOHN 4:16

May 13

Service

While your spouse is away, get the children to help you with some act of service for him. When he walks in the door, join the children in shouting "Surprise! We love you!" Then share your act of service.

August 18

Gifts

Don't wait for a special occasion. If receiving gifts
is his/her primary love language, almost anything you give
will be received as an expression of love.

May 14

Words

Psychologist William James said that possibly
the deepest human need is the need to feel appreciated.
Words of affirmation will meet that need
in many individuals.

August 17

Grace, mercy and peace from God the Father
and from Jesus Christ, the Father's Son,
will be with us in truth and love.

II JOHN 3

May 15

Time

The essential ingredients in a quality activity are:
(1) at least one of you wants to do it,
(2) the other is willing to do it, and
(3) both of you know why you are doing it—
to express love by being together.

August 16

How do we meet each other's deep, emotional need to feel loved? If we can learn that and choose to do it, then the love we share will be exciting beyond anything we ever felt when we were infatuated.

May 16

Love...always protects.

I CORINTHIANS 13:6, 7

August 15

Mercy, peace and love be yours in abundance.

JUDE 2

May 17

Gifts

Reflect on ways to give gifts to one another
even if finances are tight.

August 14

When your spouse's emotional love tank is full
and he feels secure in your love, the whole world
looks bright and your spouse will move out
to reach his highest potential in life.

May 18

Perhaps it would be helpful for us to distinguish between love as a feeling and love as an action. If you claim to have feelings that you do not have, that is hypocritical and such false communication is not the way to build intimate relationships. But if you express an act of love that is designed for the other person's benefit or pleasure, it is simply a choice.

August 13

Know therefore that the Lord your God is God;
He is the faithful God, keeping His covenant of love
to a thousand generations of those who love Him
and keep His commands.

DEUTERONOMY 7:9

May 19

Love...rejoices with the truth.

I CORINTHIANS 13:6

August 12

Time

Refuse to interrupt. Recent research has indicated
that the average individual listens for only seventeen seconds
before interrupting and interjecting his own ideas.
If I give you my undivided attention while you are talking,
I will refrain from defending myself or hurling accusations
at you or dogmatically stating my position.
My goal is to discover your thoughts and feelings.
My objective is not to defend myself or to set you straight.
It is to understand you.

May 20

Generally speaking, if we are kind and loving toward people,
they will tend to be kind and loving toward us.
That does not mean that we can make a person kind
by being kind to him. We are independent agents.

August 11

He will love you and bless you and increase your numbers.

DEUTERONOMY 7:13

May 21

Love does not delight in evil.

I CORINTHIANS 13:6

August 10

Words
___

If I choose to forgive, intimacy can be restored.
Forgiveness is the way of love.

May 22

Time

Quality activities may include such things as putting in
a garden, visiting historic neighborhoods, shopping for antiques,
going to a concert, taking long walks, or having another
couple over for homemade soup and bread. The activities
are limited only by your interest and willingness
to try new experiences.

August 9

He defends the cause of the fatherless and the widow,
and loves the alien, giving him food and clothing.

DEUTERONOMY 10:18

May 23

Love...keeps no record of wrongs.

I CORINTHIANS 13:4, 5

August 8

Look back on that point in your marriage when "reality"
set in and the initial romantic feelings faded.
How did this affect your relationship, for better or worse?

May 24

Words

We cannot get emotional love by way of demand.
My spouse may in fact comply with my demands,
but it is not an expression of love. It is an act of fear
or guilt or some other emotion, but not love. Thus,
a request creates the possibility for an expression of love,
whereas a demand suffocates that possibility.

August 7

Touch

Once you discover that physical touch is the primary
love language of your spouse, you are limited
only by your imagination on ways to express love.
Coming up with new ways and places to touch
can be an exciting challenge.

May 25

Love...is not easily angered.

I CORINTHIANS 13:4, 5

August 6

Service

Many acts of service will involve household chores,
but not all. What are some non-chore ways
of serving your mate?

May 26

Touch

Disappointments are a part of life. The most important thing you can do for your mate in a time of crisis is to love him or her. If your spouse's primary love language is physical touch, nothing is more important than holding her as she cries. Your words may mean little, but physical touch will communicate that you care.

August 5

So be very careful to love the Lord your God.

JOSHUA 23:11

May 27

Love...is not self-seeking.

I CORINTHIANS 13:4, 5

August 4

Gifts

If you are to become an effective gift giver,
you may have to change your attitude about money.
Each of us has an individualized perception
of the purposes of money, and we have various emotions
associated with spending it.

May 28

The emotional need for love is our deepest emotional need;
and when that need is being met, we tend to respond
positively to the person who is meeting it.

August 3

Time

Quality conversation requires not only sympathetic
listening but also self-revelation. When a wife says, "I wish
my husband would talk. I never know what he's thinking
or feeling," she is pleading for intimacy. She wants to feel
close to her husband, but how can she feel close to someone
whom she doesn't know? In order for her to feel loved,
he must learn to reveal himself. If her primary love language
is quality time and her dialect is quality conversation,
her emotional love tank will never be filled until he tells her
his thoughts and feelings.

May 29

Love...is not rude.

I CORINTHIANS 13:4, 5

August 2

The object of love is not getting something you want
but doing something for the well-being of the one you love.

May 30

Gifts

Gifts need not be expensive, nor must they be given weekly.
But for some individuals, their worth has nothing to do
with monetary value and everything to do with love.

August 1

But let all who take refuge in You be glad;
let them ever sing for joy. Spread Your protection over them,
that those who love Your name may rejoice in You.

PSALM 5:11

May 31

Love...is not proud.

I CORINTHIANS 13:4

July 31

Words

Love doesn't keep a score of wrongs. Love doesn't bring up
past failures. None of us is perfect. In marriage we do not
always do the best or right thing. We have sometimes done
and said hurtful things to our spouses. We cannot erase
the past. We can only confess it and agree that it was wrong.
We can ask for forgiveness and try to act differently
in the future.

June 1

What does your spouse do to make you feel more "significant"? How about what you do for them?

July 30

The Lord loves righteousness and justice;
the earth is full of His unfailing love.

PSALM 33:5

June 2

Love...does not boast.

I CORINTHIANS 13:4

July 29

What makes one person feel loved emotionally is not always
the thing that makes another person feel loved emotionally.

June 3

Service

Ask your spouse to make a list of ten things he or she would like for you to do during the next month. Then ask your spouse to prioritize those by numbering them 1–10, with 1 being the most important and 10 being least important. Use this list to plan your strategy for a month of love. (Get ready to live with a happy spouse.)

July 28

For the Lord loves the just
and will not forsake His faithful ones.

PSALM 37:28

June 4

Time

Quality activities may include anything in which
one or both of you have an interest. The emphasis is not
on what you are doing but on why you are doing it.
The purpose is to experience something together,
to walk away from it feeling "He cares about me.
He was willing to do something with me that I enjoy,
and he did it with a positive attitude." That is love,
and for some people it is love's loudest voice.

July 27

When both persons' emotional needs are met,
your marriage will take on a whole new dimension.

June 5

Words

When you make a request of your spouse, you are affirming
his or her worth and abilities. You are in essence
indicating that she has something or can do something
that is meaningful and worthwhile to you.

July 26

Let those who love the Lord hate evil,
for He guards the lives of His faithful ones
and delivers them from the hand of the wicked.

PSALM 97:10

June 6

Can emotional love be reborn in a marriage? You bet.
The key is to learn the primary love language
of your spouse and choose to speak it.

July 25

Time

If you need to learn the language of quality conversation,
begin by noting the emotions you feel away from home.
Carry a small notepad and keep it with you daily.
Three times each day, ask yourself, "What emotions
have I felt in the last three hours?" Write down your feelings
in the notepad and a word or two to help you remember
the event corresponding to the feeling.

June 7

Love...does not envy.

I CORINTHIANS 13:4

July 24

I love the Lord, for He heard my voice;
He heard my cry for mercy.
Because He turned His ear to me,
I will call on Him as long as I live.

PSALM 116:1, 2

June 8

The decision to love your spouse
holds tremendous potential.
Learning their primary love language
makes that potential a reality.

July 23

Touch

Try new touches in new places and let your spouse
give you feedback on whether he finds it pleasurable or not.
Remember, he has the final word.
You are learning to speak his language.

June 9

Love is kind.

I CORINTHIANS 13:4

July 22

Gifts

If you discover that your spouse's primary love language is receiving gifts, then perhaps you will understand that purchasing gifts for him or her is the best investment you can make. You are investing in your relationship and filling your spouse's emotional love tank, and with a full love tank, he or she will likely reciprocate emotional love to you in a language you will understand.

June 10

Touch

In a time of crisis, more than anything, we need
to feel loved. We cannot always change events,
but we can survive if we feel loved.

July 21

How can we speak each other's love language when we are full of hurt, anger, and resentment over past failures? We are creatures of choice. Poor choices in the past don't mean that we must make them in the future. Instead we can say, "I'm sorry. I know I have hurt you, but I would like to make the future different. I would like to love you in your language. I would like to meet your needs." I have seen marriages rescued from the brink of divorce when couples make the choice to love.

June 11

Love is patient.

I CORINTHIANS 13:4

July 20

Turn to me and have mercy on me,
as You always do to those who love Your name.

PSALM 119:132

June 12

Gifts

Almost everything ever written on the subject of love
indicates that at the heart of love is the spirit of giving.
All five love languages challenge us to give to our spouse,
but for some, receiving gifts, visible symbols of love,
speaks the loudest.

July 19

Words

We cannot erase the past, but we can accept it as history.
We can choose to live today free from the failures of yesterday.
Forgiveness is not a feeling; it is a commitment.

June 13

Time

In addition to the basic love language of quality time,
or giving your spouse your undivided attention,
there is another dialect called quality activities.

July 18

See how I love Your precepts;
preserve my life, O Lord,
according to Your love.

PSALM 119:159

June 14

Love is not the answer to everything, but it creates a climate of security in which we can seek answers to those things that bother us. In the security of love, a couple can discuss differences without condemnation. Conflicts can be resolved. Two people who are different can learn to live together in harmony. We discover how to bring out the best in each other. Those are the rewards of love.

July 17

Meeting my wife's need for love is a choice I make each day. If I know her primary love language and choose to speak it, her deepest emotional needs will be met and she will feel secure in my love. If she does the same for me, my emotional needs are met and both of us live with a full tank.

June 15

The man who loves God is known by God.

I CORINTHIANS 8:3

July 16

Service

Make a list of all the requests your spouse has made
of you over the past few weeks. Select one of these each week
and do it as an expression of love.

June 16

Words

The way we express desires is all-important. If they
come across as demands, we have erased the possibility
of intimacy and will drive our spouse away. If, however,
we make our needs and desires known in the form
of a request, we are giving guidance, not ultimatums.

July 15

The Lord watches over all who love Him.

PSALM 145:20

June 17

No eye has seen, no ear has heard, no mind has conceived
what God has prepared for those who love Him.

I CORINTHIANS 2:9

July 14

Time

Emotions themselves are neither good nor bad.
They are simply our psychological responses
to the events of life.

June 18

Without love, I may spend a lifetime in search of significance, self-worth, and security. When I experience love, it influences all of those needs positively. I am now freed to develop my potential. I am more secure in my self-worth and can now turn my efforts outward instead of being obsessed with my own needs. True love always liberates.

July 13

The Lord lifts up those who are bowed down,
the Lord loves the righteous.

PSALM 146:8

June 19

Love does no harm to its neighbor.
Therefore love is the fulfillment of the law.

ROMANS 13:10

July 12

Ultimately, comfort is not the issue. We are talking about love, and love is something you do for someone else, not something you do for yourself. Most of us do many things each day that do not come "naturally" for us. We discover the primary love language of our spouse, and we choose to speak it whether or not it is natural for us. We are not claiming to have warm, excited feelings. We are simply choosing to do it for his or her benefit.

June 20

Let no debt remain outstanding,
except the continuing debt to love one another.

ROMANS 13:8

July 11

My son, do not despise the Lord's discipline…
because the Lord disciplines those He loves,
as a father the son he delights in.

PROVERBS 3:11, 12

June 21

The need for significance is the emotional force behind much of our behavior. Life is driven by the desire for success. We want our lives to count for something. We have our own idea of what it means to be significant, and we work hard to reach our goals. Feeling loved by a wife or husband enhances our sense of significance.

July 10

Touch

Whatever there is of me resides in my body.
To touch my body is to touch me.
To withdraw from my body is to distance yourself
from me emotionally.

June 22

Touch

Almost instinctively in a time of crisis, we hug one another. Why? Because physical touch is a powerful communicator of love.

July 9

Words

Forgiveness is an expression of love. "I love you.
I care about you, and I choose to forgive you.
Even though my feelings of hurt may linger,
I will not allow what has happened to come between us."

June 23

Time

One way to learn new patterns is to establish a daily
sharing time in which each of you will talk
about three things that happened to you that day
and how you feel about them. I call that the
"Minimum Daily Requirement" for a healthy marriage.
If you will start with the daily minimum, in a few weeks
or months you may find quality conversation
flowing more freely between you.

July 8

Gifts

There is an intangible gift that sometimes speaks
more loudly than a gift that can be held in one's hand.
I call it the gift of self or the gift of presence.
Being there when your spouse needs you speaks loudly
to the one whose primary love language is receiving gifts.

June 24

Service

Print note cards with the following:
"Today I will show my love for you by…"
Complete the sentence with one of the following:
picking up the clutter, paying the bills, fixing something
that's been broken a long time, weeding the garden.
(Bonus points if it's a chore that's been put off.)
Give your spouse a love note accompanied
by the act of service every three days for a month.

July 7

Surely it is You who love the people;
all the holy ones are in Your hand.

DEUTERONOMY 33:3

June 25

May they be brought to complete unity
to let the world know that You sent Me
and have loved them even as You have loved Me.

JOHN 17:23

July 6

Love is a choice.
And either partner can start the process today.

June 26

Gifts

If the physical presence of your spouse is important to you, I urge you to verbalize that to your spouse. Don't expect him to read your mind. If, on the other hand, your spouse says to you, "I really want you to be there with me tonight, tomorrow, this afternoon," take his request seriously.

July 5

*The Father loves the Son
and has placed everything
in His hands.*

JOHN 3:35

June 27

If anyone loves Me, he will obey My teaching.
My Father will love Him, and We will come to him
and make Our home with him.

JOHN 14:23

July 4

Time

In each of life's events, we have emotions, thoughts, desires, and eventually actions. It is the expression of that process that we call self-revelation. If you choose to learn the love dialect of quality conversation, that is the learning road you must follow.

June 28

Words

Love makes requests, not demands. In marriage…we are not
perfect to be sure, but we are adults and we are partners.
If we are to develop an intimate relationship, we need
to know each other's desires. If we wish to love each other,
we need to know what the other person wants.

July 3

A key thought is the idea of speaking our mate's love language whether or not it is natural for us. Why do you think this is so fundamental to a healthy marriage?

June 29

Whoever has My commands and obeys them,
he is the one who loves Me.
He who loves Me will be loved by My Father,
and I too will love him and show Myself to him.

JOHN 14:21

July 2

A new command I give you: Love one another.
As I have loved you, so you must love one another.

JOHN 13:34

June 30

Love is not our only emotional need.
Psychologists have observed that among our basic needs
are the need for security, self-worth, and significance.
Love, however, interfaces with all of those.

July 1